Old CAMBUSLANG

by
Rhona Wilson

D1170447

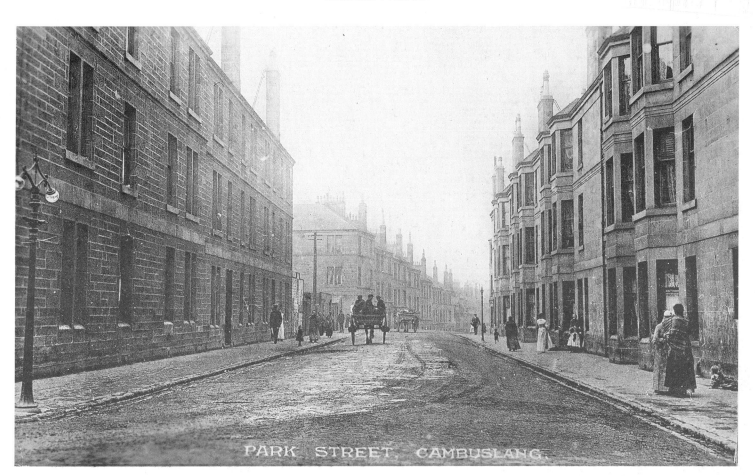

PARK STREET, CAMBUSLANG.

Park Street circa 1907.

© Stenlake Publishing Ltd. 1996

First Published in the United Kingdom, 1996
by Stenlake Publishing Ltd.
Telephone: 01290 551122
www.stenlake.co.uk

ISBN 1 872074 79 0

The publishers regret that they cannot supply
copies of any pictures featured in this book.

Although there doesn't seem to be much to drink in this parched picture of the Borgie, an old Rutherglen saying states that:

A drink o' the Borgie,
A taste o' the weed,
Sets a' the Cams'lang folks wrang in the heid.

Well, Ruglonians had to account for the number of half-wits in their neighbouring district somehow, especially after the conversions of the Cambuslang Wark.
Whatever the properties of the rivulet (also known as the Kirkburn), it is credited with the origins of Cambuslang's name. There are various theories regarding this (and whether in fact it has Gaelic or Welsh origins), but the gist of them is that *cambus* means 'bending water' and *lang* means 'bank', giving 'water with the bending bank'. It's thought that the Borgie got its name from Covenanting times when it was used as a trysting place, although this picture shows it attracting wee boys rather than religious dissenters.

Known as the 'Yill (Ale) Minister' because of the ability of his sermons to fill the pubs, the Rev. William McCulloch showed little promise at the start of his ministry in 1731. But in 1742, when Cambuslang's population was a mere 1,000, an estimated 30,000 people visited the village to hear the Kirkhill Church minister preach alongside Methodist George Whitefield. The movement, known as the Cambuslang Wark, began when McCulloch was forced to give outdoor sermons because of the dilapidated state of the parish church. Locals requested additional weekly sermons which eventually became daily, and dramatic conversions occurred (with accompanying convulsions, nosebleeds and bodily pain). Sceptics thought McCulloch's popularity might be coloured by the fact that men and women were being encouraged to spend all night out in the fields 'listening', while others considered it 'the work of the devil'. Whatever the explanations it seems incredible that someone who was initially so unsuccessful could inspire such cult-like popularity, and dominate events that are still talked about 250 years later.

IN THE PARK, CAMBUSLANG.

B.5767.

Part of the swing park, seen here in 1952, was converted into allotments during World War Two, when evacuated children were coerced into helping out in them as part of the war effort. Kirkhill Church, in the background, dates from 1840 and was built on the same site as earlier church buildings. Decorations on the roof show the shields of church heritors, including the Duke of Hamilton. The previous church, built in 1743, replaced the dilapidated building which led to the outdoor sermons of the Cambuslang Wark.

Howie's Hill, Cambuslang.

Howie's Hill was named after another troublesome Cambuslang minister, Mr John Howison, who served the parish from 1580 to 1618. He opposed the King in the fight over the establishment of Episcopacy and was jailed several times for his outspoken beliefs, doing a three year stretch on one occasion. Howison was popular for his work in the parish, and around 1603 founded Cambuslang's first public school. His 'hill', seen here about 1908, has been built over and he is now remembered by Howie's Hill Road instead. The landscape has changed so much that locals couldn't identify the location of this picture.

MAIN STREET FROM EAST, CAMBUSLANG.   B.5759.

The Auld Cellars pub, photographed in 1952 when still in business, was formerly the site of the village coal pit. In 1787 the Duke of Hamilton brought a Newcomen steam engine to Cambuslang, which was used to drain water and haul coals up from the mine and allowed deeper mining than before. However, after a fatal accident the pit closed. During an inspection, the foreman was lowered into the pit by his son, the engine man, but the works and shaft had been flooded overnight and he drowned. It proved impossible to pump the pit clear of water and it was filled in around 1800.

The construction of railways in the Cambuslang area began in 1845. In 1848 the Caledonian Railway routed its Carlisle – Glasgow line through the district, although Cambuslang Station didn't open until the Motherwell – Rutherglen route began operating in 1849. A new and bigger station was opened in 1881, and the station buildings seen here were removed in the 1960s.

The buildings on the left-hand side of this picture of Main Street were demolished in the 1960s, and Rosebank Church (seen here prior to the addition of the clock tower) was swept away along with the rest of the street at the same time. A little further down the road from the railway station is the Station Cafe, established in 1928 and still going strong. It was opened by Fred Pontiero, who arrived in Cambuslang from southern Italy in 1920 at the age of seventeen. His first job was selling ice cream from a barrow around the town for a relative who had another cafe up the street. The Station Cafe flourished even when Fred was interned on the Isle of Man during World War Two, and was used as an air raid shelter by the family during the Clydebank Blitz. Fred died in 1992 and the cafe has been run by his son (of the same name) for the past twenty-five years.

The Silverbanks area, off Glasgow Road and near to Bothwell Street, has been completely redeveloped and is now the site of modern flats. Wellshot Quarry was in the vicinity and produced stone for many buildings in Cambuslang during the nineteenth century. It stopped production around the beginning of the twentieth century but there were other quarries in the area, including a freestone quarry opened in 1876 on the Westburn Estate by Messrs Murray of Dumfries. This produced stone for building in Kirkhill and eventually became part of the public park when it closed in 1914.

It looks as if a fire drill or rescue operation is being carried out in this picture of Cairns House, taken *c.*1920. Built in the 1850s by John P. Kidston, owner of the Cairns Estate, the house was occupied by various Cambuslang industrialists. One of its previous residents was T.P. Kidston, owner of the Rosebank Dye Works off Bridge Street. The works covered a massive eighteen acres and employed many women in the area, with workers summoned at 6 a.m. each morning by the infamous bell. The factory used turkey red dyeing, one of the first innovations in textile chemistry, and the yarn produced was sold to the Indian and home markets. The works closed around 1945 and the buildings are now split between different firms.

ARDOCH GROVE CAMBUSLANG

Each side of this street has its own name. Ardoch Gardens is on one side and Ardoch Grove, which once accommodated quaint thatched cottages like the one seen here, on the other. According to one local the Grove was for the rich folk and the Gardens for the commoners!

Wellshot House, Cambuslang

Wellshot House was built up the hill in 1806 by John More, a cashier in the Royal Bank in Glasgow. The building is still standing in Milton Avenue and has been converted into flats.

Kirkhill Station was built in 1900 as part of the Cathcart Circle. Originally, the Caledonian Railway intended the line to connect the collieries and steel works of Lanarkshire with the port of Ardrossan, although this ambitious scheme was never realised. The station actually opened in January 1904 with steam trains using it until the Kirkhill – Newton section was electrified in May 1962. Opening of the line further encouraged the influx of Glasgow business people wanting to escape the dirt and pollution of the city, and building took place throughout the Villa Village to accommodate them. In 1908 a bizarre society called the Kirkhill Cronies was set up by people who travelled daily from Kirkhill by rail. Membership, which was by invitation only, was confined to eighty-five people and potential candidates had to live within a precise set of boundaries. It's not known what happened to the society – perhaps some Cronies survive who could tell us. The platform buildings have now been removed.

GREENLEES ROAD, CAMBUSLANG.

Greenlees Road *c.*1906. The farmer and his cattle have just passed Cambuslang Institute, a grand establishment that developed from humble beginnings. In 1885 the Cambuslang Social Union began when Edward Gillespie held a meeting in Main Street for those interested in setting up a social and educational centre. By 1890 the union was so successful that its committee set about raising funds for a building, and enough donations were received to establish the Institute. As the centre of community life it performed a variety of functions, ranging from a venue for World War One recruitment programmes, to town library and dance hall. The Institute has been run by South Lanarkshire Council since April 1996 and is still the focal point for pursuits as diverse as spiritualism and aerobics.

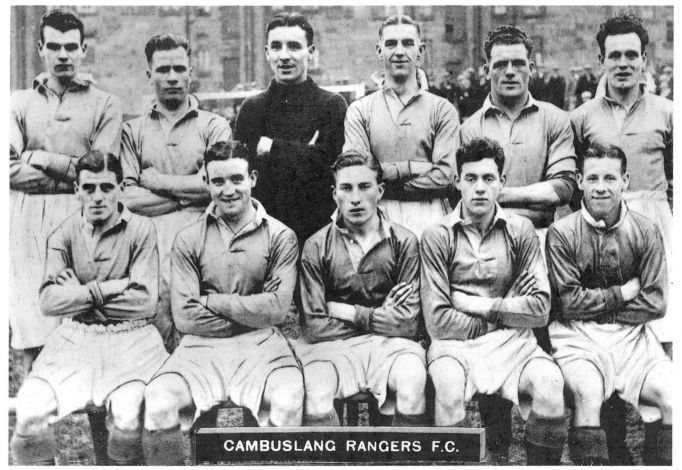

CAMBUSLANG RANGERS F.C.

These Villa Villagers are named as follows:

Back row: T. Stewart, W. Hutton, J. Clark, J. Boyd, J. Kenmuir (Capt.), R. Low.
Front row: D. Reid, T. Goldie, W. McNeil, T. Brown, R. Nutley.

Cambuslang has had numerous different football teams over the years, but the longest lasting has been Cambuslang Rangers, who formed in 1899. Amongst their many successes, they have won the Scottish Junior Cup in 1937, 1969, 1971 and 1974. Since 1904 their home has been Somervell Park, which was purchased outright by the club in 1941. They swept the board and gained a full trophy cabinet in 1971, prompting adulatory headlines from national newspapers.

The Clyde's Mill Power Station at Carmyle was built in 1916 on the site of the former Clyde Valley Power Company Station. Previous to this the area was home to a meal mill (shown here) used by farmers in the district. In the 1950s the power station was the largest in Scotland.

RIVER CLYDE, CAMBUSLANG

B 5761

The two cooling towers of the Clyde's Mill Power Station (photographed in 1952) were demolished in February 1977, just prior to the closure of the plant.

Main Street, prior to the redevelopment of the 1960s. When Mr James Allan opened Cambuslang Shopping Precinct on 2 July 1965 he was quoted by the *Herald* as feeling 'as tall as a 14 storey block of flats'. It's difficult to empathise with him. Even newspapers of the time reporting positively on the Brave New World of Scotland's sixties planners adopted an uneasy tone on mention of Cambuslang. The *Herald* stated flatly that the newly opened town centre was 'no architects dream'.

MAIN STREET, CAMBUSLANG.

At one stage Cambuslang had the highest proportion of slum houses in Lanarkshire. A survey carried out after the Second World War revealed that out of 2,500 houses 76% shared a toilet while 50% had no bathroom at all. The central area of Cambuslang was densely populated with estimates of 400 people to an acre. Obviously something had to be done, although it remains to be explained just what the town did to deserve what it got in the sixties.

SHOPPING PRECINCT, CAMBUSLANG.

The main elements of the development were the upgrading of Main Street into a dual carriageway, with the demolition of one whole side of it to make way for the precinct. Throughout frequent visits to Cambuslang I have never seen it in anything other than the isolated glory shown here. Low quality shopping units are sandwiched below low quality housing, surrounded by whimsically named multis – Sherry Heights, Rosebank Hall, Stonelaw Tower – harking back to a well and truly demolished past.

The old Co-op building, with its bowler hat roof, is visible in the distance in this picture of Main Street and still stands today. This picture illustrates particularly well how much Main Street was widened during the redevelopment. The two sides of the road seem to almost converge whereas Main Street now follows a straight line with a fair amount of space on the left-hand side. Before 1965 there would have been shops along both sides of the street as far as West Burn on the left and the Toll Pit (Hamilton Road/Croft Road junction) on the right.

Main Street in the early 1920s, busy with shop assistants, tradesmen and shoppers. The largest village in Scotland first began to grow significantly in size with the development of light industries such as cotton work and muslin weaving in the late eighteenth century. Later population expansion arose through the commercial success of Rutherglen's close neighbour Glasgow, which provided opportunities for trade plus an influx of commuters. Over the course of the nineteenth century the population leaped from just 1,500 in 1801 to 9,500 in 1881. Ten years later it had soared to an incredible 15,000, continuing to rise until it stabilised at around 26,000 in 1921.

MAIN ST CAMBUSLANG.

The population increases were of course due to establishment of the new heavy industries, and the resulting employment they brought to the area. This had a knock-on effect on the town centre, and Main Street accommodated a large number of extremely high standard and specialised shops, capable of being supported by the local economy and in turn making the town a more attractive place to live.

A reasonable percentage of the postcards illustrated in this book were published by the local firm of Peddie & Company. The lady with the shawl is just passing their shop – long since demolished – which has some of the extensive range of postcards they published on display in the window.

Andrew Park's Pastry Bakers and Confectioners shop in Main Street, *c.*1925.

Cambuslang's Cross disappeared during the redevelopment, and Kyle Court and the kiosk now stand on the site of Scoulars Ironmonger's (on the left corner in this picture). Having traded in the town for many years, the Scoulars gained notoriety for less savoury reasons when a member of the family was convicted of murdering two women in the 1980s. The turn-off for Greenlees Road is to the right, and tenements on this side of Main Street have survived reasonably intact. Station Square stood west of the cross and various orators – politicians, ministers and quack doctors – once gathered there in search of an audience. The Cross Clock is still at the top of one block, above the Clock Inn.

Although the sixties Main Street development made the largest impact on Cambuslang town centre, it could be said that the advent of trams caused the first changes. They arrived on 2 December 1903 when Glasgow Corporation Tramways extended the route from Farme Cross, and at that time the old Hamilton Road was demolished and rebuilt on a higher level to accommodate them. In 1911 the route became the Cambuslang to Anniesland line, and in 1945 the Knightswood/Kelvinside and Springfield Road services were extended to the district, although this only continued for four years. A night service from Queen Street which started in 1943 had a similarly short run when it was stopped in 1946 to be replaced by the motorbus. The last tram (No.255) left the district on 4 November 1956 for Dalmarnock Depot. The No.17 service was also cut back to Farme Cross at the same time.

The collieries in Cambuslang, particularly those in the Wellshot area, were said to be the oldest in the Glasgow area, and the writer of the First Statistical Account of the parish in 1799 estimated that mines had been worked in the district since the fourteenth century. By the time of the Second Statistical Account in the 1840s, the Duke of Hamilton's mines were rented by James Farie of Farme Castle in Rutherglen. At that time the number of men employed in the mines in Cambuslang had risen from around sixty-two to one hundred. The Third Account of the 1950s gave information on the collieries' demise listing its casualties at that point: Wellshot, Dechmont, Loanend, Toll Pit (dismantled in 1906 after thirty-one years) and Gilbertfield, amongst others. The Toll Pit (above) was situated in Hamilton Road at the junction with Croft Road.

HAMILTON ROAD, CAMBUSLANG.

This contrasting view, taken as little as forty years later, shows the effects of earlier redevelopments in Cambuslang. Nothing remains of the pit and part of its site has been built on. Today, little remains to suggest that Cambuslang once had a multitude of collieries and associated ancillary industries.

THE TERMINUS, CAMBUSLANG.

This picture was taken near St Andrew's Church at the end of Main Street, and shows the old Empire picture house at Sauchiebog (known as the 'Bug House') on the left. Other cinemas in the area were the Ritz, and the Savoy in Main Street which is now a bingo hall. Movie goers in the 1930s might have gone to see Marlene Deitrich in Blue Angel, Mae West in She Done Him Wrong or the Marx Brothers in Duck Soup. The buildings on the right have been demolished, and during the sixties development some small flats were built at Christie Place for the elderly.

The Clyde Bridge, Cambuslang.

M. 111

The Clyde Bridge was built *c*.1892 beside the old wooden Orion Bridge, which carried mineral traffic from local ironworks and burnt down in August 1919. When it was built, the Clyde Bridge was the only vehicular crossing between Bothwell and Dalmarnock. Previously, traffic crossed the Clyde at fords – when currents would allow. A notice announcing the bridge's closure appeared in local papers in 1990, although it still stands rusted, neglected and closed off at either end, surrounded by Cambuslang's eerie industrial sites. A new footbridge has been built to one side of it, while traffic crosses further up the river near to the Clydeford Road roundabout.

CAMBUSLANG FROM CLYDE BRIDGE

B 5757

The Hoover Factory stands in Somervell Street, near to the Clyde Bridge. Famous for vacuum cleaners, Hoover once manufactured wiring systems for RAF bombers, and moved to Cambuslang from London in 1943 for strategic reasons. Over 33% of all aircraft used during the war contained a part made in the Scotland plant. After the war the company resumed its commercial operations, expanding dramatically during the 1960s and 70s. In 1974 the plant occupied a million square feet, and in the early 1980s an astonishing 6,000 people worked there. Despite being hit by recessions, the plant has survived and in 1993 profited when the company chose to transfer around 500 jobs from their Dijon plant to Cambuslang. However, Hoover will most likely be remembered for its flights promotion fiasco in the early 1990s. The company promised – some say recklessly – free transatlantic flights with selected Hoover products and were then surprised by the high response. The rest is history!

THE OLD MILL CAMBUSLANG.

At one point there were two corn mills in Cambuslang (one on the Calder and one on the Clyde) which were used by farmers in winter and spring and by Glasgow grain dealers for the rest of the year.

According to the Third Statistical Account, there were around six smithies in Cambuslang at the turn of the century. They were often attached to coal pits, although by the 1950s there was only one pit blacksmith, and two private smithies at Cathkin and Dalton. One blacksmith's shop stood behind the old Empire cinema.

This picture and the one opposite show farriers at work in the Cambuslang area. The one on page 34 was most likely taken at the smithy, although this picture was probably taken at a local farm. But which one?

This 1920s picture shows the Cambuslang division of the St Andrews Ambulance Association. The ambulance was probably built at Scott's of Bellshill. One of the first medical services in the district was provided by workers from Hallside Steel Works who paid a weekly amount towards a General Practitioner. The group only disbanded in the 1980s.

This view of Hamilton Road, taken in the late twenties or early thirties, is unrecognisable today. The road is now a dual carriageway with Christie Place to the left and the shopping precinct to the right. The old Borgie Rest, Swiss Rest and Athletic Bar can be made out in the background.

Hamilton Road at Flemington, with Hallside Presbyterian Church on the right. The tramway company was responsible for the part of the road in which its tracks were laid, and as a result the middle of the road was always better maintained that the edges, which the County Council was responsible for. A baker's van from Gilchrist's Woodlands Biscuit Factory in Hamilton stands on the left of this picture.

Another of Gilchrist's vans, photographed somewhere between Cambuslang and Hamilton, *c.*1905.

Long before the National Grid and large public power utilities, towns and cities in Scotland were responsible for generating their own electricity. Many private companies operated small power stations (the Lanarkshire Tramways had their own power station in Motherwell), as did some of the County Councils. Around the turn of the century, the County Council established a refuse destructor and electricity generator in the Silverbanks area of Cambuslang. The authorities pushed the project through, despite the opposition of local businessmen who thought the neighbourhood would be overrun with disease and fumes (the plant did incinerate household waste, after all).

Initially, the new plant generated electricity for use in Main Street and for private consumers up the Hill. By 1912, street lighting was extended to Flemington and the electricity generated was used for private consumption as well as street lighting in Cambuslang. The works were managed by William Love, a close friend of another Cambuslang worthy, Sir Thomas Lipton. Lipton, the famous yachtsman, resided in Johnstone Villa and set up a chain of grocery shops before going on to buy up tea plantations.

HALFWAY, CAMBUSLANG.

As a place name Halfway is all too revealing, suggesting that the village serves as a milestone *en route* to somewhere else. Gilbertfield Co-op was situated on the corner of Hamilton Road and Glen Street in a purpose-built shop dating from 1894. When this picture was taken in the mid-thirties, there were reasonable shopping opportunities within the district, and some locals from Cambuslang-proper used to travel to Halfway to go to dances in the tiny Ebenezer Hall. Along with much of Cambuslang, the area was redeveloped by the 1960s planners. The buildings directly across from the Co-op have been demolished (replaced by three-storey flats and the Tudor Inn) and Hamilton Road widened. The main centre of Halfway is a rundown and depressing row of shops. Although some attempts have been made to revitalise the area and to create a sense of community (with the establishment of the library, for instance), the atmosphere of the village remains insular and neglected.

WELLSIDE BLDS. HALFWAY CAMBUSLANG.

Most Halfway locals I asked about this picture were completely stumped as to its location – not surprising considering the whole block has been demolished. The tenements, which were bounded by Craigallan Avenue and Wellside Drive, have been replaced by a modern block where Halfway Library stands now.

In the distant past there were possibly as many as seventy or eighty small farm steadings similar to this one at The Deans, scattered over a wide area, particularly to the east end of the parish. One author states that as late as 1884 there were primitive roofless houses still to be seen in this area. The Duke of Hamilton hastened the development of Cambuslang by his policy of consolidating small crofts into extensive farms, a process that was encouraged by the growth of new industries which provided alternative employment for displaced agricultural workers. 'The Deans', seen here c.1904, has been replaced by Deans Avenue – two rows of distinctly suburban semi-detached houses.

Hamilton Road from Halfway, 1905. The building directly opposite Crawford's pub housed the Co-op and is still standing, although everything in the picture above has disappeared. Further along the road is the Sun Inn, which was probably serving ale when this picture was taken. According to locals, it has been in existence for at least one hundred years.

Lightburn Road at Newton Burn *c*.1912.

Hamilton Road, Halfway *c*.1912.

Hallside Steel Works were established in an attempt to use up a by-product from the St Rollox chemical works in Glasgow. They extracted sulphur from pyrite and were left with tons of a substance nicknamed Blue Billy. Charles Tennant of the St Rollox works thought it might be possible to use the waste material for the production of steel, and teamed up with Charles Siemens (who was busy developing blast furnaces) to form the Steel Company of Scotland in 1872.

Hallside, belonging to the Duke of Hamilton, was one of the few Lanarkshire locations which fitted all the criteria necessary for production; it was a level site of between 70-100 acres, had a good water supply, plus rail links to ports and the iron and coal districts. The establishment of the works in this isolated area meant that workers' accommodation and other amenities had to be built from scratch. Houses and tenements, a shop, church, school, tennis courts and allotments were all established there.

Unfortunately for Tennant and Siemens, Blue Billy proved useless in experiments, although techniques developed at the new works laid the foundations of Scotland's steel industry. The company's first order was for 1,000 tons of steel rails for the Caledonian Railway, and it subsequently produced steel plates for the expanding shipbuilding industry. (The first ocean-going steel hulled steamer, the *Rotomahana*, was built in 1879 with steel from Hallside). By the end of the 1880s steel plates and girders for the Forth Rail Bridge were being produced at Hallside. In 1920 a group of shipbuilders actually bought the works to guarantee their supply of steel.

Hallside was sold to Colvilles in 1936 after a two year period with Sir James Lithgow. Despite intentions to shut the factory down, it was granted a reprieve by the advent of World War II when around 2,000 people worked round the clock to produce shells, bombs and tank parts.

In 1960, Hallside was cleared of all equipment with the exception of the foundry facilities, and re-opened as part of Clyde Alloy Steel producing alloy steel billets. The works were nationalised in 1967, and six years later the workforce had dropped to 546. The factory's closure was announced on 12 December 1979. Today, the abandoned ground looks like a landfill site and is the subject of a research project into land regeneration. Special trees and worms are being used in an attempt to detoxify it.

TELEGRAPH OFFICE

HALLSIDE POST OFFICE.

MONEY ORDER OFFICE
POST OFFICE
SAVINGS BANK

G R
POST OFFICE
LETTER BOX

Hallside is named after the great hall of Drumsargard Castle, which at one time stood on a site adjacent to Hallside Road. Stones from the castle were used to build the farm houses which originally made up the village. This post office, provided for employees from the nearby steel works, opened *c.*1912 and closed on 16 December 1963 as the industry declined. Gilbertfield Post Office in Halfway is now nearest to the district.

The meeting point of the Clyde and Calder, with the chimney and winding gear from one of the collieries at Newton in the background. The sender of this postcard thought that the view was 'lovely', and would have been familiar with collieries – there were two near to her home in Polmaise, Stirling, where the card was sent to.

It's difficult to identify the buildings in this 1910 picture of Newton Brae because the street has changed so radically. If the whitewashed building on the left-hand side is the Newton Inn then all the other buildings have been demolished, some replaced by modern villas. St Charles' Primary School is out of picture further down the street on the right. The Inn itself is boarded up and for sale – but no takers so far.

Newton Public School stood along from Newton Farm Road, next to Layton's grocery shop. After closing, the school was used as a store until an arson attack destroyed it around 1958. Today the only school in Newton is St Charles' Primary, which celebrated its centenary in 1993.

FARM INDUSTRY, GATHERING POTATOES. BRANDON SERIES

John Spier held the tenancy of Newton Farm from 1876 until his death in 1910. Hugely interested in agricultural innovations, Spier influenced practices even outwith Great Britain – King Haakon of Norway made him a Knight of the Order of St Olaf in recognition of his achievements, which included work on the elimination of tuberculosis in cattle, and the introduction of new crops. In 1886 he pioneered the use of hay-making machinery on his own farm using the rick-lifter and horse-fork. This enabled ricks of hay to be brought in from the field and throw up onto the stack using horse power. The potato crop being gathered in this picture was an important part of the farm's production. Although gathering was done by hand the digging was carried out by a machine which increased production by 200%.